Metamorphosis

Mina Hayat

BookLeaf
Publishing

Presentation by *BookLeaf Publishing*

Web: www.bookleafpub.com

E-mail: info@bookleafpub.com

ISBN: 9789395026604

First edition 2022

Letters to self

I write letters
to my old-self,
to be read
by my future-being.

Pain

How do I silence my aching heart
Every broken piece screams pain
Why do I find solace in this anguish
When all it does is drive me insane

A forlorn heart

In the deepest silence of the night
The walls seem ghostly quiet
Surrounded by people yet all alone
With a broken heart, I sit and mourn
Lies and deceit, right from the start
He released blackness into my heart
Lost in sinful bliss that flowed into me
I was too blind to see all it did to me
Sadness, sulking, sufferings..
Never did he notice my offerings
Bringing my parts together which are fragile
I write this poem which is but futile

World full of illusions

She couldn't fathom how he could make her feel
so vulnerable
His tantalizing touch, a touch so tender
Passion, madness and dreamlike surrender
His voice and his words held her captive
In a World full of illusions and magic

Sweet love

5

You awakened and destroyed
my soul so beautifully..
I'm amazed at how your sweet love
could cause so much destruction

Garden of love

In our garden of love..
I pick roses full of thorns and
Shed my leaves as I take a stroll,
O' darling..
Forgive me if my words prick your soul.

Ocean of lies

I told you I was drowning
You lend me a hand only to push me
Further down in your ocean of lies

A love tragedy

I find myself lost in
night-long laments
without you..
This forlorn heart of mine
swims in oceans so deep
without you..
Our love is nothing but a good tragedy
The way I live with you
But,
without you.

Moon love

Sheltered by your moon love
I flew away from the sun
like a mourning dove,
Starlit sky
Illuminated lies,
Brooding duskiness
and deep sighs,
Forever lost
in heated hazes
and twisted mazes.

A drunken stupor

Your remembrance
my endurance,
Unspoken wounds
my utterance,
Silent cries and
notions that lie,
A drunken stupor
in deep reverence

Heartache

The heartache you gave me
I carry it in my bones
and every inch of my skin
like a sin

Why?

You wash away all the pain
only to come back and
hurt me again
Why..
Do you care so much
to take me to the sky then leave me hanging in
the air so high ?

Your name

I have sadness inside my body
pain flowing through my veins
to areas in my brain
where I keep your name

Ocean of truth

It was only when I dived
deep into the ocean of truth,
I was able to measure
the depth of your lies

Brightest star

15

She walks into darkness
and her soul shines
as the brightest star
in the darkest night

Fragile warrior

I am a fragile warrior
I fight with my brokenness

Inherited pain

Why do I carry
the burden of my ancestors
and pay for sins
I made never

Letting go

I don't want to hold onto you
the longer I do
the more I lose

Metamorphosis

She was drawn to the light of the sun and when
she discovered she had wings, she
metamorphosed into a butterfly.

Grief

Grief is important,
for healing
for growth
for changed mindset
for feelings so true
for a newer YOU

Best lesson

You were the best lesson learnt
despite the pain and the hurt